MARGIN OF
DEATH

MARGIN OF
DEATH

HOW CLOSE
WE COME EACH DAY

DEJI BADIRU

MARGIN OF DEATH
HOW CLOSE WE COME EACH DAY

iUniverse books may be ordered through booksellers or by contacting:

iUniverse
1663 Liberty Drive
Bloomington, IN 47403
www.iuniverse.com
844-349-9409

Cover Illustration By Dudu Emmanuel, Lagos, Nigeria

ISBN: 978-1-6632-6294-3 (sc)
ISBN: 978-1-6632-6293-6 (e)

Print information available on the last page.

iUniverse rev. date: 05/20/2024

Books in the ABICS Publications Book Series
(www.abicspublications.com)

1. **Margin of Death: How close we come each day,** iUniverse, Bloomington, Indiana, 2024.
2. **Soccer Greatness at Saint Finbarr's College (Volume II): Legacy of All-Around Sports,** iUniverse, Bloomington, Indiana, 2024.
3. **Academics, Discipline, and Sports at Saint Finbarr's College: Tributes to the Great Soccer Players,** iUniverse, Bloomington, Indiana, 2023.
4. **More Physics of Soccer: Playing the Game Smart and Safe,** iUniverse, Bloomington, Indiana, 2022.
5. **Rapidity: Time Management on the Dot,** iUniverse, Bloomington, Indiana, 2022.
6. **The Physics of Skateboarding: Fun, Fellowship, and Following,** 2021.
7. **My Everlasting Education at Saint Finbarr's College: Academics, Discipline, and Sports,** 2020.
8. **Twenty-Fifth Hour: Secrets to Getting More Done Every Day,** 2020.

9. Kitchen Project Management: The Art and Science of an Organized Kitchen, 2020.
10. Wives of the Same School: Tributes and Straight Talk, 2019.
11. The Rooster and the Hen: The Story of Love at Last Look, 2018.
12. Kitchen Physics: Dynamic Nigerian Recipes, 2018.
13. The Story of Saint Finbarr's College: Father Slattery's Contributions to Education and Sports in Nigeria, 2018.
14. Physics of Soccer II: Science and Strategies for a Better Game, 2018.
15. Kitchen Dynamics: The Rice Way, 2015.
16. Consumer Economics: The Value of Dollars and Sense for Money Management, 2015.
17. Youth Soccer Training Slides: A Math and Science Approach, 2014.
18. My Little Blue Book of Project Management, 2014.
19. 8 by 3 Paradigm for Time Management, 2013.
20. Badiru's Equation of Student Success: Intelligence, Common Sense, and Self-Discipline, 2013.
21. Isi Cookbook: Collection of Easy Nigerian Recipes, 2013.
22. Blessings of a Father: Education Contributions of Father Slattery at Saint Finbarr's College, 2013.
23. Physics in the Nigerian Kitchen: The Science, the Art, and the Recipes, 2013.
24. The Physics of Soccer: Using Math and Science to Improve Your Game, 2010.

25. **Getting Things Done Through Project Management,** 2009.
26. **Blessings of a Father: A Tribute to the Life and Work of Reverend Father Denis J. Slattery,** Heriz Designs and Prints, Lagos, Nigeria, 2005.

About the Author

Deji Badiru is a Professor Emeritus of Industrial and Systems Engineering. He is a registered Professional Engineer, a certified Project Management Professional, a Fellow of the Institute of Industrial & Systems Engineers, a Fellow of the Industrial Engineering and Operations Management Society, and a Fellow of the Nigerian Academy of Engineering. His academic background consists of BS in Industrial Engineering, MS in Mathematics, and MS in Industrial Engineering and Ph.D. in Industrial Engineering. His areas of interest include mathematical modeling, systems engineering modeling, computer simulation, and productivity analysis. He is a prolific author and a member of several professional associations and scholastic honor societies. Deji holds a U.S. Trademark for DEJI Systems Model for Design, Evaluation, Justification, and Integration.

Dedication

Dedicated to memory of all those who have been lost in road accidents.

Acknowledgements

I thank and appreciate all the readers who continue to support the titles in the ABICS Publications Guidebook series. New entries are often motivated by constructive feedback from readers. Without you, my dear readers, this book series would have been stymied after just a few titles. I particularly thank Dudu Emmanuel Studio and Kaffy Studio, both of Lagos, Nigeria, for providing complimentary drawings that depict the traffic case example included in this book. I also appreciate the thorough copyediting service provided by Ms Michaela Rose Finn on the raw manuscript. Without her keen eyes for properly dotting all "i's" and crossing all "t's," this book would not have been as exciting to read as it is now. Aye to Michaela!

Margin of Death is a cautionary note on death being a slim margin away in the activities we engage in. The book presents safety and life preservation [tips to avoid, minimize, or mitigate accidental disasters that could rob people of their precious lives. Although the topic is serious and unnerving, this book is written in a humorous tone, perhaps to put readers at ease. Life is always at risk from a variety of sources, ranging from accidental, negligent, and deliberate acts. While natural age-driven death is accepted, we should minimize exposure to other non-scheduled, life-robbing incidents, a majority of which are manmade. Doom and gloom could happen even in a time of bloom. Being consciously aware of this reality could help us with a physical, mental, and spiritual preparation.

On the natural expectation of death, Nepal's Dalai Lama says the following:

> *"Worrying about death is a waste of*
> *time. Death is a part of life."*
> – Dalai Lama

1

In essence, life and death go together, like in a continuum. We cannot have one without the other. Sometimes, they are close together, as in an unpleasant outcome. Sometimes, they are, desirably, far apart. A near miss is the one we know about, but the narrow margins are the ones we never know.

Life is a transient asset: it comes and goes. It can be gone in a flash, when least expected, and particularly when tragic events happen, such as a road accident. This written piece is motivated by a near-miss road experience that could have led to a disastrous outcome. As a prolific author, I had, for many years, harbored the idea of writing an advisory book on the "margin of death" to caution readers about the frailty of life, based on multiple incidents seen, observed, and reported in society. We tend to take life for granted, which I thought we needed to rethink. Writing about the margin of death helps us recognize and appreciate how fleeting and short life can be. The tranquility and serenity of life can be snuffed out in an instant.

This is a story of how close to death humans come each day of their lives, sometimes without knowing it. It provides facts and fiction of the narrow escapes, close calls, and near-miss events that people never know about. You could turn the corner and escape just in the nick of time, when death (by whatever means) is lurking around the corner.

For example, you are being targeted by robbers at a deserted train station in a bad neighborhood. You stand there, with no worries in the world, waiting for the midnight train. The train arrives, the door opens, you get in, the door closes. The robbers, who are hurrying to catch up with you, are locked out of the train by inches of the door closing them out. You go on with your journey, unaware of the fate that nearly befell you.

Although many dangers to life exist in all facets of human existence, the opening case example in this book is about the dangers of the roads of travel and transportation around the world. Road accidents create havoc all over the world. So much so that several YouTube channels present programs on "the most dangerous roads in the world." Such programs are tragically exhilarating, and provide cautionary notes about road travels and accidents. Unpleasantly, most of the most dangerous roads are located in developing and underdeveloped parts of the world. When roads in developed nations fall in the category of most dangerous, it is often due to road congestions, weather-related mishaps, and driver errors rather than the physical infrastructure of the roads. As more efforts are directed at making roads safer, we see more and more impaired drivers on the roads. The quote below conveys that the more efforts that are made on road infrastructures, the more danger may lurk on the roads due to the flaws of humans, who tend to take things for granted.

"The sturdier the glass, the more shatter
it makes when it breaks."
– Deji Badiru

The sensitivity highlighted in this book could help us all be more conscious of our driving habits, environments, and our individual and collective responsibilities on the roads. Each road danger presents a narrow margin of death. Therein lies the theme conveyed in the title and front cover of this book. Other quotes of relevance are shared below:

"The reality of life is death."
– Deji Badiru

"The reality of death is just a stone throw
away within a narrow margin."
– Deji Badiru

"Avoid hurried worries in harried times."
– Deji Badiru

Story telling is often an effective way to get points and guidelines across. For this reason, my writing style in this book follows my usual story telling pattern, which is popularly admired by friends and colleagues as "Deji-Vu" stories. "Deji-Vu" is a fun play on the popular social buzz of "Déjà vu," a French phrase that describes a familiarity with situations one hasn't experienced before. Some people even carry the Deji style to the full buzz of "Deji vu, all over again." Yes, even if I have told the same story again and again before, it helps the mental retention of my audience to hear the same story again. Thus, I am proud of the effectiveness of "Deji vu, all over again."

The initial story of focus in this book is a near-miss incident that my wife and I experienced in January 2024 in Lagos, Nigeria. I have had it in mind to write on the "margin of death" for many years, but I never got around to it due to conflicting priorities. The last straw that finally sparked my writing this book at this time is the incident narrated in the following paragraphs.

It was a pleasant and clear afternoon on a major road leading to the all-important bridge connecting the mainland and the Island of Lagos, Nigeria. Traffic was flowing smoothly with a diverse combination of all types of vehicles. My wife and I were in the back seats of a Jeep vehicle, driven by an experienced and attentive driver, for whom we had the affectionate nickname of "Baba Olokere." The driver's old-fashioned mobile phone invited such a humorous nickname. His phone was of a caliber below the old flip phones and he adoringly referred to his phone as "Okere," which meant "Squirrel" in functionality comparison to modern smartphones. For this, we jokingly called him "Baba Olokere," which means owner of a squirrel. He couldn't do much with the phone, but it worked for him for his most basic needs of making and receiving phone calls. Texting was a foreign capability on his phone but who needs texting when his primary function was driving? On the roads of Nigeria, like in many other countries, every day is a precarious gamble between life and death. Safety on the roads requires a driver's rapt attention. This focused attention probably saved our lives on this particular day.

This short road trip was initiated by a dinner invitation from a family friend living on the Lagos Island portion of the Lagos city megapolis, a crowded city of over twenty-three million inhabitants, according to the 2024 estimate by worldpopulationreview.com. Sixteen million are estimated to reside in Lagos proper with another nine million residing in the general urban area. It is a mega city with chaotic and jumbled road and transportation infrastructures. To make it through each disorderly road on any day is to toy with the narrow margin of death. To be fair, the same could be said about many other mega cities around the world, including Cairo, Egypt, Karashi, Pakistan, and Chicago, Illinois, U.S.A.. Traffic congestion can make any city dangerous for travelers. The higher the population density, the more horrendous the traffic profile, which, consequently, leads to travel dangers on congested roads. Headlines are equally disheartening, such as the following:

"Highway collapse leaves at least 24 dead."

"Driver found guilty in fatal bus crash."

"Bridge accident plunge workers to their death."

"A Yellow Springs man was killed in a crash Thursday evening that injured three others, including two children."

"Beavercreek couple and child killed in a crash in Kentucky." It goes on and on with devastating news of lives lost prematurely due to one type of accident or another. Some are preventable, particularly if they emanate from capricious actions.

It would have been a wide-sweeping tragedy to read a headline that says "Professor and wife die in horrendous traffic accident on Lagos road." As much as we pray and wish they wouldn't, these tragedies unfortunately still occur. Just as prevention is better than cure, it is a fact that preemption is better than redemption. We were saved and spared by our driver's fast reaction to evade the situation and prevent a potentially horrendous crash.

Our journey to Lagos Island started on the Mainland, Ikeja area, to be specific. Several family friends were invited to the august dinner reception in honor of the conclusion of the memorial lecture for the late Professor Oye Ibidapo-Obe at the University of Lagos campus. Professor Ibidapo-Obe had been a scholarly collaborator on a variety of intellectual engagements during his illustrious life. He died on January 3rd, 2021. Readers are referred to the Appendix of this book for my written tribute to Professor Ibidapo-Obe upon his demise. The second biennial memorial lecture, for which I was the keynote speaker took place on January 5th, 2024. The appreciation dinner, organized and hosted by his spouse, was scheduled for the 9th of January on the Victoria Island segment of the Lagos island. This is why we were headed to the Island from the Mainland of Lagos. My wife and I had travelled to Nigeria, specifically for the memorial lecture. I had spoken remotely via Zoom at the first memorial lecture in 2022. I had promised the family that I would attend the second memorial lecture in person to present my lecture directly on site. So, it was an obligatory travel to Nigeria.

We were just a few kilometres down the busy, but not congested, road to the Lagos Island. Everything looked smooth and safe. Our vehicle was on the outside lane, next to the concrete road median (or culvert), on a three-lane, right-hand-drive highway. Nothing looked out of the ordinary, until a pedestrian pushing a cart of construction iron road, breached the concrete median and pushed his cart that was heavily laden with iron road, in front of our vehicle, with less than six feet of road leeway to spare. Meanwhile, the traffic behind us was streaming along and bearing of us from behind. At the same time, a large commercial trailer truck was on the right side of our vehicle, on the passenger side. I was in the back seat on the passenger-side. My wife was in the back seat with me. She was seated on the driver-side of the vehicle. There was a split second shout and reaction from our driver when this immense hazard suddenly interjected itself into the flow of traffic. The driver exclamation of horror was "Yehpa!!!" which is equivalent to shouting "Oh God!" or (pardon the expression) "Shit!" At the same time that he exclaimed this unpleasant squeak, he took an unbelievable evasive move, narrowly driving through the marginal space that existed between the loaded cart right in front of us and the speeding truck on our right side. It was like an angle lifted our vehicle through the clouds to avoid a horrific collision, which would have led to an extended pile up on the busy road. We were left visibly shaken in the back seat, full of praise for the driver's immaculate driving skills and thankful for God sparing our lives. Following this near-miss experience, we remained disoriented for many days to the extent that we cancelled all our subsequent trips to the Lagos Island. The virtual representation of this incident is captured in the details provided in the front cover of this book. Readers are encouraged to take a look again at the illustrative cover. A complementing alternate illustration for the cover was provided by Kaffy Studio of Lagos, Nigeria. It is provided below for views from the front and from the back.

The Deji-vu story above is just one case example of what people experience directly in terms of a near-miss in a road traffic. There are countless similar and unrecognized near-misses, dangers fitting this book's theme of "margin of death." These can range the gamut, from petty crimes in the neighborhood that escalate to death-causing incidents to mass shootings and stabbings in public places. One such example is the testimony by a New York novelist, Paul Auster, who wrote about the "Element of Chance," in which case he narrowly missed being killed by lightening. According to his report, at the age of fourteen, he was at a summer camp, at which a boy next to him was stricken and killed by lightening. His luck of the draw was that if the lightening had been just a few inches of over, it could have killed him instead of the other boy. This was, indeed, a narrow margin of death. Sudden death, by the narrowest of margins, became a preoccupation of Paul Auster's novels, based on his own observations.

On another front, the 2024 student protests that roiled university campuses in the USA were explosive enough in some cases and could have led to someone's death. The paradox of life involves our extreme pursuits of enjoying life, only to create unrecognized opportunities for untimely death. Death is a part of the cycle of life. The continuum of life, existence, and death can be unnerving, but it is the reality of life, itself. Unanticipated hydroelectric dam collapses in Brazil, Kenya, Cameroon, and other places have caused loss of lives. These are other margins of death that rushed onto unsuspecting residents in dam areas. From a systems perspective, incidents that might, otherwise, appear to be innocuous, could lead to death. Take for example, the day the 911 emergency telephone system went out for over three hours in the USA states Nebraska, Nevada, South Dakota, and Texas. Millions of people lost the ability to reach out for emergency needs. Lives have been lost in the past in cases where 911 callers were not able to get emergency help when critically needed.

In another interesting testimony, I once saw a YouTube video where a husband wanted to play a practical joke on his wife by hiding under a pile of leaves raked from the Autumn foliage in the Midwest region of the USA. He claimed to enjoy playing harmless pranks on his wife. He timed his pile-of-leaves hideout to be just before his wife was to arrive at home from work. The plan was for him to jump out of the pile of leaves as his wife walked by the pile. He proudly announced, "I am going to jump out from under the pile of leaves and scare the crap out of her." Everything was going well, according to his pranking plan, until the phone rang and he prematurely jumped out of the pile of leaves to answer the phone call. Just as he was running towards the phone on a nearby bench, his wife came driving down the street and accelerated, deliberately, right through the pile of leaves because the pile was placed in her normal right of way to reach the driveway of their home. Only seconds separated the barreling car from the man's fortuitous escape. The man narrowly escaped by some divine intervention. That's how the lucky man navigated through a narrow margin of death. In another series of videos, multiple pedestrians are shown narrowly missing disasters on many roadside accidents. Each case was a matter of inches of separation between death and survival. The caption on the videos says, "This is why you must pray every day." Yes, prayers do help from the perspective of positive thinking about desired outcomes. But what happens in the cases of those who, indeed, die from such close-call of inches? Did they not pray fervently enough? My take on this "margin of death" theme is that, in addition to praying, we must take proactive actions to preempt disasters by being cautious of where disasters are likely to lurk.

In one personal testimony, my longtime childhood friend, Babs Ayeni, and I often recall our close call that we experienced while growing up in a neighborhood of Lagos, Nigeria. We were about ten years old then and we frequently played and pranked around the neighborhood, particularly in the afternoons, after school. One day, we dared to challenge ourselves to jump in the Lagos river to demonstrate we could survive even though neither of us could swim at that time. The daring challenge was, fortuitously, overheard by a passing-by adult, who, forcefully, dissuaded us from trying what could have meant a sure death for both of us. We are both over 70 years old now, and we still get a kick out of thinking of the stupidity that we almost embarked upon. The margin of death was narrowly averted by a passerby.

While remaining thankful for the road safety of Lagos on the 9th of January 2024, I am reminded of other road thankfulness of the past. Below is a recollection of how my family was rescued after our car broke down on the highways of Tennessee in the 1970s. The story of our mountain road rescue in Tennessee goes as re-narrated on the following pages.

Christmas stories of each Season remind me of my family's experience in September 1977 on one of the imposing mountains on I-40 between Nashville and Cookeville, Tennessee. Our older son, Ade, was born on June 10th, 1977 and, as a part of our exploration of the USA during a late-Summer break from Tennessee Tech (before the Fall quarter of those days), we decided to drive our newly-acquired jalopy car to New Orleans. It was a long, hard drive for relatively new foreign students and parents in the USA. We had a good time and a memorable experience in Louisiana.

On the drive back, we were unable to make the long journey during daylight. We considered breaking the trip into two days, but we didn't have money to stay in a hotel overnight somewhere enroute home. We could not afford even the cheapest of Motel 6 of those days. So, we decided to press on into the dark-driving night. Things went well until we were about 25 miles West of Cookeville at around ten p.m. when our jalopy car, a high-mileage 1966 Ford Custom 500, was called upon to get us up and over the last test of endurance (the mountain in question, whose name I never knew). The car promptly conked out at a point that appeared to us (at that time) to be a perilous incline like we had never experienced before. We were scared, despondent, and worried about what could happen to us overnight in an unfamiliar area, where no one knew where we were, with a three-month old child on Iswat's lap. There were no laws about seatbelts and putting babies in car seats in those days.

There we were, a young black family of three, lost in the dark in an unknown Mountain location in Tennessee. It was, indeed, very terrifying. There was no exit nearby in the desolate and frightening bushes on either side of the road. There were no cell phones in those days. It was getting cold as mountain Winter was beginning to roll in at that time of the year. Sleeping in the car overnight until we could get daylight help was not an option.

After several minutes of debating what to do next, I decided to step out of the car to see if my rudimentary, yet unproven and untested, engineering skills could be brought to bear in coaxing the car to come out of its slumber. I knew I could not do anything, but as the head of the family, I thought I should demonstrate to my family that I was, at least, trying to do something. I opened the hood, groped in the dark for one wire or another, and silently prayed that the Hands of God would guide me to the right wire that I could jingle to magically bring the car to life. Nothing happened.

Meanwhile, all sorts of paired lights whizzed by, despite the fifty-five mph Interstate speed limit of those days, blowing torrents of high-powered air that rocked the disabled car and the human occupants. Some of the passing lights were high while some were low. Since I could not make out the outlines of the vehicles, I could only guess the varying sizes of the vehicles. The hood was up and the darkness was unforgiving, so Iswat could not see me or what I was doing under the hood. Due to the ambient noise of passing interstate traffic, I could only faintly hear her calling out to me "what is it?," hoping that I would have an answer. I had none. So, I offered her no response. Besides, my lips were beginning to quiver due to the descending cold of the night and I could hardly speak.

Worried about my welfare under the hood of the car, alone, she stepped out of the car with Ade in her arms. She came beside me and stood on the road-marker side of the road shoulder as if to shield me from the vehicles zooming past our car. I continued to fidget under the hood as if knew what I was doing. Suddenly, a pair of lights that had been approaching fast suddenly slowed down, went a few yards past our location; then two pairs of lights, one pair red and big and the other white and small, started coming toward us from the opposite direction to the flow of traffic. Judging by the height of the lights off the ground, I guessed this must be a large car. We did not know what to make of it. Are they coming to help us or kill us, I questioned in my mind. Of course, I did not reveal the latter of those two thoughts to Iswat. I softly said, "Maybe we will get some help from them."

When the car got close to us, it stopped. A big elderly man and a young lady came out of the car; the man from the driver side, and lady from the passenger side on the back seat. The man started saying "Do you need . . . . .?", but before he could get in another word, he was interrupted by the young lady, who appeared to be about eighteen or nineteen years old. She exclaimed to the older man, "Dad, he is my classmate at Tech, we need to help them." I was shocked. This lady was definitely not in any of my classes at Tennessee Tech. She then asked me, "Are you going back to Cookeville? That's where my parents are taking me back to school." How she guessed that we were going to Cookeville, I never knew. It could have been because she immediately knew that we were foreign individuals, obviously of college age, and could only be heading toward the university town of Cookeville. I quickly said "Yes."

The young lady then turned to Iswat to ask "How are you and your baby?" Iswat replied "Okay." The young lady then said, "We can give you a ride because Tennessee Tech is where we are going." I replied, "Thank you, we live at Tech Village," the university housing for married Tennessee Tech students. Nodding her head in the direction of her father, the young lady appeared more excited by saying "they are taking me to my residence hall at Tech." Meanwhile, the father had no chance to say anything. The young lady did all the talking and negotiation. Leaving all our travel items in our disabled car, we hopped in the back seat of the large car and sat beside the young lady, who resumed her previous seating location in the car. An older lady was in the front passenger seat. She politely greeted us and welcomed us into the car. The car pulled back out onto the Interstate and we happily rode with this unknown family toward Cookeville.

It was during the ride that we learned what prompted the family to stop to help us in the first place. The young lady was moved by the sight of seeing someone holding a baby on the side of the Interstate in such a cold, dark, and remote place. She urged her parents to stop and help. Based on that account, I concluded that in her sympathetic urge to help, she must have lied to her parents, on the spur of the moment, that she recognized me as a classmate. It was the greatest helpful lie ever told. I was further convinced of this because the young lady did most of the talking and never once mentioned anything about the class that we were, supposedly, taking together. If she was my classmate, she would have mentioned something about our class together.

Stunned by the family's unsolicited help, Iswat and I kept quiet throughout the twenty-five-mile drive, except for occasional responses to inquisitive questions posed by the young lady and the older lady. "What is your baby's name?" "Where did you travel to?" "How long did you drive?" On we went until we were dropped off at our Tech Village apartment. We thanked them and bade them farewell. Iswat and I were just within two years of coming to the USA from Nigeria, so the pull of our culture of deference to elders precluded us from asking for the names of the family. In our culture, which we still find difficult to pull away from, it is an extreme disrespect to ask an older person for his or her name. What are you going to do with the name? Call the person by name? That's a no, no. Thus, we never learned anything about this very generous and caring family. The family probably voluntarily offered their names, but the names never registered with us in our moment of anxiety. This is something I still regret until today.

Very early the next morning, Mr. Bassey Udosen, one of the other Nigerian students at Tennessee Tech, and I went in his car to attempt to rescue and retrieve my disabled car. Mr. Udosen was a Mechanical Engineering student and was well versed in tinkering with mechanical things. We got to the car and it was still intact. All our travel items were still in it. It appeared to be none the worse for wear. Not trusting what would happen, I opened the door, inserted the ignition key, and cranked the engine.

Miraculously, the car roared to life without any under-the-hood prompting. It must have been driven long and hard the previous day to the point of some component getting overheated and "tired." It was not the radiator because that would have signaled its distress with a flash of steam or fire. I drove the car back to Cookeville without any incident. Mr. Bassey Udosen followed me in his own car to ensure that my car did not pull any other surprises. I arrived home safe and sound. Thus, we ended the harrowing experience with a Jalopy Car. We never took another long trip in that car for as long as we owned it. We remain eternally thankful for the help offered to us by the nameless family. The preceding story is composed in a thankful recollection. Had we not been rescued by the gracious family, we could have, perhaps, faced a precarious margin of God knows what.

Related to social linkages are cases where the neglect of social responsibilities could lead to criminal activities that could lead to someone's death. Such margins of death exist in many communities and should not be taken for granted. I once wrote about this type of community linkage in a short piece in the past. The socially focused essay is echoed below as a social responsibility commentary of why community wingman ship should be Every day for everyone. We are all in the same pot of a social mess. When the pot is stirred, we all end up in the messy mix; and what goes around comes back around to touch every one of us. It is the responsibility of each one of us to take action and make contributions in the early stages to preempt bigger social problems later on; and prevent being personally touched by socially derailing crimes later on.

The report of a past Florida school shooting brings up an important issue and the necessity for community wingman ship. It has happened again. Mass shootings in schools, churches, meetings, offices, and what have you. It is a sad, sad epoch of human existence. The recurrence of these acts of violence points to the need for more wingman ship efforts toward everyone every day. This is important, not just within the military, but also within the entire society.

Our lives are more intertwined than we want to believe. What goes around in one place comes around everywhere else. Whenever a horrific act like this happens, we clamor for one remedy or another, including more gun control. However, that is just one piece of the system of systems of remedies. One aspect that is often ignored is the need for earlier watchfulness and preemptive wingman ship. We need to direct more efforts toward preemptive measures that can prevent resorting to mass violence. We often ask for the motive for such an act. Of course, we never know for sure, but one thing that is clear is that delusionary feelings of despondency can lead a person toward total disregard for life, of self and of others. The military ethos and culture of wingman ship, if applied broadly within the external community, have a lot to offer in terms of making everyone develop a feeling of belonging.

In this context, wingman ship is everyone's social responsibility and should be practiced daily. There is a need for everyone to take on the social responsibility for everyone else, particularly the youth. The adage that "it takes a village to raise a child" has never been truer than in the present days of social uncertainties. Social stability and advancement of our society is everyone's responsibility. We cannot afford to look the other way whenever we notice something that is not right or something that does not bode well for the welfare of the entire society. Social issues that we fail to address now may magnify into incidents that could adversely touch everyone in society, directly or indirectly. As individuals, we owe it to ourselves and our community to participate in the resolution of societal problems actively and directly. There is so much decadence evolving in modern society. Many of these deplorable social issues manifest themselves in the form of criminal activities brought on by feelings of frustration, disenfranchisement, isolation, depression, desperation, and hopelessness. When members of our community are noticed to be facing mental stress, financial discomfort, and despondency, it behooves all of us to offer helping hands. The extension of help can help preempt serious problems later. If we do not help, minor problems may become big felonious incidents that may come back to touch us in unanticipated ways.

A community may think it is safe by cocooning itself within the security walls of its neighborhood, but the reality is that no one can be completely insulated from problems that occur within the community. With freedom of movement and closing of geographical gaps, crime importation and exportation should be a big concern for every one of us. We should all share in the collective responsibility of helping to preempt the evolution of social decadence so that we don't have to deal with the results later. It is obvious that prisons have become a huge drain on society. Whether we want to accept it or not, we all pay for prisons. We pay in terms of loss of human capital, loss of loved ones, impedance of economic growth, and the opportunity cost of the loss of a productive workforce. Wouldn't it have been cheaper to institute programs that would preempt criminal tendencies and, consequently, reduce the need for more prisons? For social ills, preemption is far better than incarceration. Programs that help to forestall crime are often cheap, subtle, and innocuous; such as offering social support to the less fortunate, providing a basis for optimism in youth, creating an atmosphere of belonging for everyone, offering encouragement, projecting empathy, and facilitating educational opportunities. For youth, support, discipline, and comfort are as much a responsibility of the parents as they are of everyone in the community. We are not all too far removed from the possible adverse impacts of juvenile delinquency. Education and support systems are sure ingredients for advancing society and minimizing criminal acts and horrific incidents. We should all practice Wingman ship every single day of every year toward everyone.

Another interesting story from my Deji-vu collection is my fictional encounter with a tree. As much as we adore and admire trees, sometimes an encounter with a tree could be deadly, fitting the definition of a margin of death.

The USA Occupational Safety and Health Administration (OSHA) reports that on average, there are over 100 landscape and tree-related fatalities every year. Within the tree care industry, these numbers are even higher. In fact, the tree care industry is one of the most dangerous in America. In a Philadelphia blog not long ago, the law firm Reiff presents an opinion that of all nature's flora and fauna, trees seem to be among the very safest. After all, trees cannot sting or bite us. They can't lay eggs in our floorboards, or peck and scratch at our vulnerable flesh. They can't enter a cut to give us an infection, and they can't bite down on our ankles and drag us beneath the surface of the ocean. They seem harmlessly anchored deep in the ground, still and serene for all time. However, while it's true that trees are perfectly safe in the vast majority of instances, it *is* possible for trees to pose a danger along the line of a margin of death. It may be a bizarre accident which can only be attributed to natural forces or a matter of negligent maintenance involving carelessness and liability.

It was mid-July, the height of the typical rainy season in Tennessee. I had gone to an administrative meeting and was walking back to my office along a tree-line pathway. A beautiful, tall, eastward leaning tree caught my attention. Somehow, I looked at the tree suspiciously. I don't know why. Something was playing mysteriously in my subconscious mind. The evening news the previous night had reported several downed trees in my neighborhood because of the evening's thunderstorms. My mind must have been wondering innocently why this tree was still standing despite the abuse it must have suffered over the years. As I walked past the tree, I eyed it curiously but cautiously, as if to say, "I'm watching you." Suddenly, the tree started to fall in my direction as if my untrusting staring instigated a retaliatory action from the tree. I froze instantly. This was due to two reasons that I did not appreciate at the time.

One half of my immobilization was due to fright. The other half must have been due to a deliberate calculated move to determine what the tree was going to do before I made my own move. It is amazing how quickly the mind races through thoughts in moments like this. Thoughts and rationalization that would have taken hours to untangle quickly became clear. While still standing frozen, I thought if I moved too soon, the tree would figure out my intention and it would change its course to come after me viciously. So, I waited until the split second when I knew the tree could no longer change its course. I jumped off its falling course. In my younger and more pliable days, I would have jumped at least six feet off the tree's course, but my limbs have lost much of their elasticity in recent years. So, I could manage only a couple of feet of hop. Whammm, whammm, whammm, the tree smashed into the ground. Although the main trunk missed me, I could not escape the malicious lashings of the branches. Flashes of the lashes that those in medieval servitude must have felt came to my mind. What a terrible ordeal.

I sheepishly picked myself up from the ground after being sent on my knees by the "crazy" branches. Long and telling streaks of open flesh lined my body. I asked myself. How am I going to explain to anyone that a tree did this to me? My wife certainly would not believe me. She has always accused me of telling tales; just because I am an imaginative writer. My children would surely find this amusing. I have always chastised them not to get into any whipping encounters. "Avoid troubles so that you don't come home with scratches," I have always told them. It would seem that I have not lived up to my parental preaching. I thought of hiding until all the evidence had healed but knew that would not work. I was expected home soon, and I would risk close inspection once my tattered clothing was noticed. I thought of going to the store and buying new coveralls, butut that would not work either because it was a hot summer period and coveralls would run counter to my normal summer attire. Finally, I concluded that the right thing to do was to tell the truth as it was. Everyone would be understanding and supportive once they heard my plight. I thought I would put a humorous start to the story to put listeners into a good sympathetic mood. So, upon getting home, I told my wife how a tree beat me into a pulp. Her terse response was that I should have been sucked into the pulp of the tree. So much from a compassionate companion. To make a short story long, I did not get the domicile sympathy that I deserved and anticipated. To be tongue-lashed after being tree-lashed is quite humiliating. I'll have to watch out more closely for falling trees next time. For their own part, the leaning trees are watching me, ever more ominously.

Here is another piece that is a satire on a "pack of lies" related to flight delays. This comes to mind because there have been instances where flyers were saved by missing doomed airplane flights, in the avoidance of a margin of death. Of course, the reverse has also happened. Anyway, here goes the pack of lies parody. It starts with an innocuous announcement.

"If you're on Flight 881 going to Knoxville, we've just been notified of a ten-minute delay," a muttering of an outer-space alien voice announced over the airport Intercom air waves. Voices coming from far-off alien space often get down to Earth distorted.

"Sir, what did she just announce," I asked a fellow flier, who seemed to be a seasoned Cosmo traveler himself.

"The tower just announced a ten-minute delay," he reassured me.

That's not bad, I opined. With the *good* weather we're having, I was expecting worse . . . . like a one-hour delay.

Ten minutes later, I walked over to the counter, "Are we taking off now? . . . . It's been more than five minutes past the ten minutes announced earlier," I inquired with subdued humility. The counter, in its inanimate best, reiterated the earlier reassurance that we would be taking off soon.

Thirty minutes later, the inevitable was announced . . . . five to ten more minutes. *Okay, I can deal with that,* I thought. The announcer continued . . . "We'll get you there as fast as we can and safely." Yah, that air of safety concern that soothes and pacifies irate passengers. We all kept quiet . . . . now seemingly lethargic to the incremental announcements.

One hour later, I summoned enough courage, walked over to the counter . . . again. "Are we making progress toward departure?" This inquisitive query elicited an account of the source of the delay . . . . in a whisper. "We don't want to panic passengers or anything like that; but the pilot is arriving on another flight coming in from Frankfurt. We'll depart as soon as he rushes through immigration and customs." Poor fellow! He will have to race from the international concourse to get to the regional wing just to make sure we are not delayed any longer. He will be all ruffled up, probably sweaty from the intra-airport run.

Finally, thirty minutes later, the pilot arrived, walked briskly to the counter, showed his badge, and is waved onto the aisle leading to the cockpit. I watched him closely, monitored his relaxed strides, and marveled at his quick recovery from a stressful intercontinental flight and the dash from gate to gate.

Anticipating departure, I packed up my belongings that had, by now, worked their ways onto adjacent seats, creating a defensive buffer between me and neighboring passengers. Nothing happened for several more minutes.

Thankfully, we boarded twenty minutes later.

Then, "Welcome on board," a flight attendant announced. "This flight is completely full, make sure all your belongings fit in your overhead bin and please sit in your own seat. I'm sorry we're so full . . . you will not be able to change seats on this flight." We all complied. Being a self-imposed compliant conformist, I reined in all my wayward belongings and made room for my in-bound seat mate.

Now comfortable, I shut my eyes and dozed off. The backward jerk of the plane woke me up as my packed-in elbow flayed uncontrollably into the next seat. "Excuse me, ... I am sorry," I murmured in my sleep-induced stupor. My seat mate did not respond. I opened my eyes, turned my head to make an apologetic eye contact. I saw right through him straight onto the next row of seats. Just then, the flight attendant, all primed up like a flying angel, came down the aisle.

Packing in my shoulders to signify my earlier compliance, I asked her, "Where's my seat mate? I made room for him you know." She looked intently into my eyes and just snickered.

I got the message . . . . it's all a pack of airtight lies.

In multiple scholarly journal publications, authors have addressed many reasons for traffic accidents, as summarized below. Every year, road accidents claim the lives of millions of people and cause countless injuries worldwide. These accidents not only result in personal tragedies but also impose a heavy economic burden on individuals, families, and society as a whole.

Insurance companies have vested interests in minimizing road accidents and, thereby, reducing their liabilities. Studies by insurance companies have resulted in tips and guidelines for reducing accidents. While accidents can occur due to various factors, it is crucial to understand the auto insurance components of responding to road accidents, thereby promoting safer driving habits and mitigating risks. Insurance companies have delved into the most prevalent causes of road accidents and the ensuing insurance implications. According to a release by a coalition of European insurance companies, some common causes of accidents are summarized in the paragraphs that follow.

Distracted Driving

In recent years, distracted driving has become one of the leading causes of road accidents. With the proliferation of smartphones and other electronic devices, drivers are increasingly tempted to engage in activities like texting, talking on the phone, checking social media, or even watching videos while behind the wheel. These distractions divert their attention from the road and significantly increase the chances of an accident.

Speeding

Excessive speed is a major contributor to road accidents. When drivers exceed the speed limits, they compromise their ability to react to sudden changes in road conditions, increase the braking distance required, and reduce the effectiveness of vehicle control. Speeding not only endangers the driver's life but also puts other road users at risk.

Drunk Driving

Driving under the influence of alcohol or drugs remains a significant cause of road accidents. Intoxicated drivers experience impaired judgment, reduced reaction times, and decreased coordination, all of which makes them highly susceptible to causing accidents. The solution to this problem lies in responsible behavior, which means refraining from driving after consuming alcohol or taking any substance that impairs one's ability to operate a vehicle safely.

Reckless Driving

Reckless driving encompasses a range of dangerous behaviors on the road, including aggressive maneuvers, tailgating, running red lights, and changing lanes without signaling. Such reckless actions often lead to collisions and severe injuries. Practicing defensive driving techniques, which involve anticipating and responding to potential hazards, is crucial in avoiding accidents caused by reckless drivers.

Poor Weather Conditions

Inclement weather conditions such asheavy rain, snow, fog, or ice make roads slippery and decrease visibility, significantly increasing the likelihood of accidents. These adverse conditions require drivers to adapt their driving techniques accordingly. Slowing down, increasing the following distance, and ensuring adequate visibility through the use of lights and wipers are essential precautions to prevent accidents caused by poor weather conditions. Additionally, staying informed about weather forecasts and planning travel accordingly can help minimize exposure to hazardous weather.

According to some car insurance coalition releases, despite taking precautionary measures, accidents can still occur due to various factors. Precaution is an ultimate path to better road protection and survival. In such unfortunate events, having adequate insurance coverage can provide financial protection and peace of mind. Car insurance policies cover damages to the insured vehicle, medical expenses, and liabilities arising from accidents. It is crucial to select a policy that suits individual needs and preferences, considering factors such as coverage limits, deductibles, and additional benefits like roadside assistance or rental car reimbursement.

According to auto insurance companies, understanding the common causes of road accidents is essential for promoting safer driving practices and reducing the risks associated with travelling on dangerous roads. By recognizing the dangers of distracted driving, speeding, drunk driving, reckless behavior, and other risk factors, individuals can adopt responsible driving habits that prioritize road safety. Citizens are encouraged to practice more responsible driving. Some guidelines provided by insurance companies are summarized below:

1. **What should I do if I encounter a distracted driver on the road?**

   If you notice a driver who appears distracted, it is important to maintain a safe distance from their vehicle and avoid any aggressive actions. Focus on your own driving, be cautious, and give the distracted driver plenty of space. If necessary, you can report the incident to local law enforcement with details such as the license plate number, location, and a description of the vehicle.

2. How can I prevent accidents caused by poor weather conditions?

To prevent accidents in poor weather conditions, it is crucial to adjust your driving behavior accordingly. Reduce your speed, increase the following distance between vehicles, and use headlights and windshield wipers appropriately. Stay informed about weather forecasts before travelling, and if the conditions are severe, consider postponing your trip if possible.

3. What should I do if I suspect a driver is under the influence of alcohol or drugs?

If you suspect a driver is impaired by alcohol or drugs, do not attempt to confront or engage with them directly. Instead, keep a safe distance and promptly contact local law enforcement, providing them with as much information as possible, including the vehicle's description, license plate number, and the location and direction of travel. Reporting such incidents can help prevent potential accidents and protect other road users.

4. What role does defensive driving play in preventing accidents caused by reckless behavior?

Defensive driving is a crucial skill that helps anticipate and respond to potential hazards on the road. By practicing defensive driving, you can better identify and avoid reckless behavior exhibited by other drivers. It involves maintaining a safe following distance, being attentive to your surroundings, and being prepared to react quickly and safely to unexpected situations.

5. **How can I handle an encounter with wildlife while driving?**

If you encounter wildlife on the road, it is essential to stay calm and avoid sudden movements or swerving, which can cause a loss of control. Slow down and honk your horn to alert the animals, giving them an opportunity to move away. If a collision with wildlife is unavoidable, prioritize your safety and try to minimize the impact by braking firmly and maintaining control of your vehicle.

Workforce preservation has been a focus of interest for me for many years. The interest arises from the realization that untimely deaths, due to accidents or nefarious human activities, do rob a nation of its vital human resources. One of my past writings in this is reprinted here, specifically in the context of workforce development and preservation for national renewable energy strategies and implementation, for the case of Capacity-Building needs for the proactive adoption of renewable energy and energy efficiency in Nigeria.

As the nation of Nigeria is now worrying and agitating about the future of energy in the country, with a particular focus on switching to renewable energy, it helps to remind ourselves of the long-ago quote by Winston Churchill:

"Let our advance worrying become
advance thinking and planning."
– Winston Churchill

This quote was uttered in the wake of the World War II worrying that pervaded the entire world. What we are facing these days is akin to a world war on the future of energy. The Renewable Energy Committee of the Nigerian Academy of Engineering (NAE – Nigeria) has been tasked to ruminate and strategize on how the nation could develop strategies for moving towards renewable energy. Among several topics being tackled by the committee, members of the committee are specifically charged with addressing the topic of **"Capacity Building Needs for the Active Adoption of Renewable Energy and Energy Efficiency in Nigeria."** Therein lies my submission tendered herewith.

I have been focused on workforce preservation in Nigeria (and elsewhere) as a result of an unfortunate incident that I witnessed in Nigeria in 2000 (See Attachment I). My approach to making a contribution in this regard leverages a rarely-addressed theme of workforce preservation. Workforce, in this sense, relates to "manpower development or capacity building" in the usual parlance of developing nations. My argument in this approach centers on the need to not only "build capacity," but to also "preserve capacity." If you build capacity, you must preserve it for it to provide a meaningful result for the nation. People constitute the primary capacity of a nation. Thus, any effort about building capacity must also address a commitment to preserving (i.e., keeping safe) the capacity (i.e., people) that has been developed. Whatever the strategy might be for transitioning to renewable energy, people will, ultimately, be responsible for implementing the strategy. What happens if the people educated, trained, and groomed to lead the renewable energy initiative are not available to execute the charge due to being vanquished by a lack of safety and security in the nation. We often make the mistake of believing that highly-trained personnel (e.g., engineers, policy makers, decision makers, managers, movers and shakers) will always be there and available to deliver the goals and objectives of renewable energy. This is a fallacy, as my testimony narrated fully in Attachment I would reveal. The genesis of the testimony is that I witnessed the life of a highly-educated professional being snuffed out of existence by an incident of armed robbery. I came to the realization that all efforts to educate, train, and prepare this particular professional for national development went for nothing, all because his life could not be preserved. For all of us, no matter how Interested, Willing, and Available (IWA) we think we are, our lives could be in jeopardy in a flash, if safety and security are not assured. Please read Attachment I to get the full background story of my approach to this strategy-development task.

Too often, we focus too much on the provision of technology (e.g., ICT: Information and Communications Technology) to get things done. Unfortunately, we often neglect the process and the people involved. If the process is flawed and the people are not protected and preserved, no technology can solve our problem. The nexus of achieving goals and objectives in renewable energy and other pursuits revolves around technology, people, and process. People, as the constituents of the workforce, are very essential and must be preserved. We should invest in renewable energy workforce development and preserve the people constituting the workforce for renewable energy.

There is an urgent need to broaden the national communication channels related to renewable energy programs and initiatives. Most often, we (engineers, researchers, professors, and intellectuals) preach to the choir among ourselves. Rarely do we engage with the general public on the issues of renewable energy, its importance, and relevance to our general wellbeing and future survival. The general public represents the bulk of the population required to adopt renewable energy practices. But rarely do we engage the general public in public-service and public-awareness programs to promote renewable energy. Here, I present my Triple C (communication, cooperation, and coordination) framework for getting everyone on board for project goals and objectives. This framework is recommended for the nationwide push towards renewable energy. The Nigerian Academy of Engineering can step forward to be the conduit for sensitizing the general public to the benefits and urgency of converting to renewable energy. Badiru (2024) leverages the Triple C framework for pushing efforts to reengineer our actions to influence our environmental world positively. Increasing participation through direct involvement will pay dividends in having more people to embrace renewable energy more broadly. The lesson from Confucius is applicable here, as echoed in the quote below:

> "Tell me, and I forget;
> Show me, and I remember;
> Involve me, and I understand."
> – Confucius (Chinese)

The more we communicate the terms and requirements of renewable energy to the general public, the more people can get involved and the better they can understand. In this regard, bi-directional communication pathways will embrace bottom-up and top-down communication streams. A clear communication leads to personal cooperation, which leads to the coordination of individual actions. Theme: Get more of the public to be aware and knowledgeable about renewable energy. Some pertinent questions that can be included in the Triple C communication of renewable energy include the following:

- What is the purpose of renewable energy?
- What exactly is required of each participant?
- Why is renewable energy required?
- What is the urgency of renewable energy initiatives?
- Who is in charge of the national drive for renewable energy?
- When is a conversion needed?
- What is the cost of converting?
- Who will bear the cost?
- How is an ordinary consumer going to participate in renewable energy?

Communication should be bi-directional, covering the different stakeholders, including federal level, state level, local level, institutional level, community level, company level, neighborhood level, household level, and personal level. Downward the upward flows of communication (in both directions) should be embraced.

This section is an adaptation of one of my workforce-centric articles, with a refocused emphasis for the current era of workforce development, as it might relate to renewable energy programs post-COVID-19. The workforce disruption caused by COVID-19 necessitated a new focus on the challenges of workforce development around the world. The decimation of productive human resources caused by

COVID-19 requires not only the traditional strategies of workforce development, but also the uncharted territory of workforce redevelopment and preservation. The reports we are getting indicate a precipitous decline in the ability of the workforce to continue to contribute to economic development and vitality of a nation. When businesses open back up, it will be necessary for workers to relearn their jobs to return to the level of proficiency and efficiency needed to move the economy forward. The technical topic of learning curve analysis postulates that performance improves with repeated cycles of operations. Whenever work performance is interrupted for a prolonged period, as we experienced during COVID-19, the processes of natural forgetting or technical regressing set in. To offset this decline, direct concerted efforts must be made beyond anything we have experienced before. This led to our call for new innovations in workforce development and redevelopment. We cannot be lackadaisical in leaving things to the normal process of regaining form, routine, and function. In the present era, return-to-work programs should consider efforts to reorganize for renewable energy, particularly related to the mode and frequency of transportation. Work-at-home programs may alter renewable energy practices. It is the **recommendation** of this section that rigorous research and policy studies be conducted within the context of workforce interfaces for renewable energy.

Typically, we erroneously focus on technical tools as the embodiment of workforce development. More often than not, process innovations might be just as vital. Workforce development, in particular, is more of a process development than of a tool development. There are numerous human factors aspects that can enhance the goals of workforce development. Some of the innovations recommended here include paying attention to the hierarchy of needs of the worker, recognizing the benefits of diversity, elevating the visibility of equity, instituting efforts to negate adverse aspects of cultural bias, and appreciating the dichotomy of socio-economic infrastructure. While not too expensive to implement, these innovative strategies can be tremendously effective in the push for renewable energy. To tie this to the earlier discussion of workforce preservation, it should be noted that "safety" is one of the critical needs of the workforce. Safety, as earlier argued, directly impacts workforce preservation. A workforce member eliminated by a COVID impact or other safety-related incidents is a workforce member that we fail to preserve. Typically, the society addresses safety and security as necessary social mandatesMy **recommendation** here is that we need to elevate that perception to the level of workforce necessity for workforce preservation.

As one cliché emanating from the COVID-19 pandemic has taught us, "we are all in this together." To this end, we must all reengineer our actions for the purpose of advancing workforce development, such that renewable energy initiatives could take hold. Skilled workforce is the cornerstone of national development. However, the pursuit of manpower development without measures of preservation is analogous to building a national foundation on quicksand. Without risking a loss of generality, let us accept "manpower" as an idiosyncratic term referring to both men and women. For this reason, I often use "manpower" and "workforce" interchangeably. All sectors of the Nigerian economy proclaim their dedication to workforce development with the fervor of a trumpeter. Nowhere is it ever mentioned that workforce preservation is just as important as its development. Workforce development without a preservation strategy symbolizes a non-holistic view. Without a preservation strategy, any development effort is bound to fail. The neglect of workforce preservation pervades both the public and private sectors; and it is obvious that the neglect of preservation strategies is one reason that our national development continues to flutter. For Nigeria to advance, there must be an urgent development of a strategy to preserve whatever workforce is developed.

I have had opportunities to participate in various workforce development initiatives in Nigeria over the past two decades. During all the strategic deliberations, not once was workforce preservation mentioned as a co-requisite for workforce development. A recent tragic event instigated my urge to write on this issue at this time. Many concerned citizens have written and offered suggestions about policies and actions needed to solve pervasive problems in Nigeria. There is no shortage of ideas. There is no shortage of passionate and eloquent rendition of solution strategies. What is lacking is the will, ability, and dedication to implement the solutions. For this reason, I, at first, hesitated to write this article. I did not want to clutter the newsprint with yet another set of grandiose ideas devoid of action. However, this case is significant enough that I can risk grandiosity, with the hope that some action might follow. As a concerned citizen, I see it as my obligation to bring this plight to the attention of other citizens. Every one of us knows of at least one "developed" workforce that has been brutally eliminated from the nation's workforce pool. Thus, leaving a long train of family agony and national deprivation. We can hardly imagine the level of opportunity cost incurred because of lost workforce. I suspect that some of the difficulties faced in revitalizing some sectors of the economy may be due to the frequent loss of trained, developed, experienced, and valuable workforce. We all recognize recyclable brain drain as a national concern. Permanent workforce drain is more devastating. This reality, unfortunately, receives less attention.

The case in point is that of the late Mr. Al-Hassan Alasa, who was recently cruelly eliminated from the nation's workforce pool by armed robbers. Mr. Alasa might not have been a celebrity in the usual sense of the word, but in my mind, he is a public figure, whose case deserves widespread public knowledge. Nigeria lost a gem of a gentleman.

I met Mr. Alasa at a training session at TCC (Training and Conference Center) Ogere. He made such an impression on me during the first few minutes that I felt as if I had known him for a long time. We discussed, among other things, technical workforce needs in Nigeria, changes in society, democracy, political and business advancements in Nigeria, as well as the new banking systems in Nigeria. We discussed the new service initiatives available at his bank (Standard Bank and Trust). He pointed me to the bank's new website, which I subsequently enjoyed visiting. Banking, Mr. Alasa's profession, has advanced tremendously in the past few years since the crop of professionals, like Mr. Alasa, came into the industry. If he had been allowed to continue his life, he would have made far more contributions to the banking industry and the nation. Unfortunately, the people of the underworld did not allow him. What a waste of a national resource!

I was so distraught about Mr. Alasa's death that I was not myself for several days. I kept hoping that the sudden news would turn out to be a hoax. To my chagrin, the news checked out after I reconfirmed with another mutual friend of ours. I had innocently sent him an email, not realizing that the forced hand of death had descended upon him. Being away from the country, I had not heard the news about his encounter with armed robbers. After several weeks of not hearing back from him, I inquired from an acquaintance of his. Thus, came the sad news. I can only imagine what this loss would have meant to his family, his co-workers, his industry, and all those who had the good fortune to have known him. It is a devastating loss to everyone; a lingering pain.

Mr. Alasa's case is one of many cases that combine to remind us how fragile the pillars of workforce development could be. Several organizations spend millions of Naira for personnel security within and around company premises. What happens beyond company premises is an errant display of insecurity. Workforce assets that are preserved while at work become vulnerable in the open community. Many valuable employees are lost during encounters on the roads and private homes. To make matters worse, prospective workforce pools are cruelly mauled down before they can be cultivated.

New (even radical) approaches may have to be explored to preserve our workforce assets.

One strategy that is worthy of consideration is the pooling of security resources to provide a blanket of protection for citizens at work, on the road, and at home. This essentially requires always making the nation safe for all. I refer to this concerted effort as Security Synergy, which provides a more effective security program than the individualized and localized efforts of separate organizations.

National security, personal safety, and personnel preservation are essential for a sustainable national development. How can security synergy be achieved nationwide? This will require voluntary and consensus agreement among companies. Strategic communication, cooperation, and coordination are the hallmark of developing and maintaining national safety for the purpose of workforce preservation. If the business environment is safe, the business climate will be stable, and companies can thrive and contribute to national development programs.

A sort of voluntary security levy or corporate donation can be solicited and dedicated to the provision of an integrated security program under the auspices of existing national security forces, but under the trusteeship of a committee of company security representatives. This will help mitigate the frequent complaints about lack of governmental resources to provide adequate security. Why should companies embrace this sort of additional burden on their meagre revenue base? Well, it is a matter of interest in workforce preservation and cost effectiveness. Preservation of trained workforce makes economic sense for a company. In addition, pooling of security resources, if carefully orchestrated and managed, can provide more widespread benefit for all; thereby, reducing the risk and burden associated with individualized programs.

The memory of lost loved ones, such as the late Al-Hassan Alasa, necessitates that we act on workforce preservation and minimize the adverse impacts of the margin of death. May God give us the strength to pursue the correct solutions.

Appendix 1

Tributes and Lessons from the Life of Professor Oye Ibidapo-Obe

By
Professor Adedeji Badiru

I still find it hard to believe that my scholarly partner and research buddy is gone. Gone forever. This is a sad twist of life. The only comfort I can derive from this sorrowful event is that Oye lived his life his own way, but left an indelible positive mark on the society. His lessons of life will continue to benefit humanity for ages to come. His untimely death is a monumental loss for the scientific and engineering communities around the world. Yes, around the world, because Oye touched many parts on the world and left his scholarly imprints everywhere.

Our intertwined stories of educational, scholarly, and administrative collaborations go back to when we first met at the First Africa-USA International Conference on Manufacturing Technology (MANUTECH) at the Sheraton Hotel in 1993. Over the next 1,400 weeks until his death, we communicated almost every other week. On October 30th, 2020, he sent me a text message to inform me that he and Professor Ayo Ogunye were online to attend my Lifetime Award investiture by Taylor & Francis. On November 26th, 2020, he emailed me about his search for a reputable book publisher for the manuscript he was working on about the History of Ijeshaland. We exchanged several text and email messages on that topic for several days, during which period I informed him that I also was thinking of writing a personal account on Epeland, where I hailed from. My wife and I suspected something might be amiss on December 25th, 2020, when I sent him a special WhatsApp message about my wife's 65th birthday and I never got a response back from him. The next day, my wife asked me if I had heard back;I said "no" and put off the question by suggesting that our world-traveler Oye might be out of the country and could not get my messages. I sent him another generic email message unrelated to the birthday inquiry just to check if he was following any of his messages. I never received a response. The shock of my life came on December 31st, 2020, when my nephew in Dallas, Texas, Mr. Olu Durosimi, a close friend of Oye's son, Bambo, called me to deliver the sorrowful news. I prayed that it was a cruel hoax. Alas, it was true. I was shocked, drained, disoriented, and sleepless for the next two days. My last WhatsApp message to him is frozen permanently at 8:30am (USA Eastern Time), on December 25th, 2020.

I have spent countless hours since then reflecting on how closely tied I had been to Oye's scholarly pursuits over the past 27 years. Professor Oyewusi Ibidapo-Obe was so intellectually curious and scholarly restless that he drew everybody around him into new technical pursuits. His favorite words included systems, control, research collaboration, innovation, development, technology, and other technically challenging lexicons. Although he was an exceptionally accomplished professor, each new opportunity to collaborate made him look like a kid in a candy store. He was excited about everything. He never declined any opportunity to collaborate intellectually. Upon all of these, he was a simple man with simple needs. Amidst our many social pleasantries, we engaged in many, many high-level ruminations on how to use our scholarly tools to facilitate a sustainable development pathway for Nigeria. He was an ardent patriot and ambassador of Nigeria's development and advancement.

Oye had a unique talent of working with diverse cadres of people both horizontally and vertically. This ability enriched his life and made it possible for him to go anywhere and interact professionally in multiple ways. When I was at the University of Oklahoma, he presented a distinguished guest lecture, and we ended up creating a Unilag-OU International Academic Exchange Program. When I was at the University of Tennessee, he presented another distinguished guest lecture, which led to the creation of a Unilag-UTK International Academic Exchange Program. It was through this partnership that Associate Professor Sunday Asaolu came to the University of Tennessee as an exchange scholar. When I moved on to the US Air Force

Institute of Technology, Professor Ibidapo-Obe presented a seminal paper at a high-profile Air Force symposium on the topic of mathematical modeling for emergency response operations. He carried the banner of Unilag so widely and prominently that an American colleague of mine at AFIT referred to him as "Professor Unilag," probably because he could not pronounce Ibidapo-Obe.

His technical worldwide contributions, for which I had first-hand knowledge, could span a multi-page manuscript. For the purpose of this brief tribute, I point to only a few of his scholarly products, as conveyed pictorially on the following pages. We wrote two books together, in collaboration with our dear friend, Dr. Babs Ayeni. The cover images of the books are included in the embedded photo below. Also, in the cover images are the two Festschrifts written on Professor Ibidapo-Obe, one at Unilag and one at FUNAI. He insisted I must contribute chapters to the festschrifts, which I did. In his characteristic altruistic simplicity, he ceremoniously autographed a first copy of the Unilag festschrift to me.

There could never be another professor of the same caliber of Professor Oyewuse Ibidapo-Obe. Earlier on, on May 3rd, 2020, Oye sent me an outline of a new book he wanted to write. Echoed below is what he had in mind:

"Big Data, Fuzzy Models, Systems Controls and Artificial Intelligence Simplified with Applications"

1.0 Introduction

2.0 Big Data

What is Big Data-the Law of Large
    Numbers (Smirnov-K)
BDA (Big Data Analysis-Statistics and
    Inferences, Missing Data)
Big Data and IT and AI
The transformation journey From Big Data
    through AI to ETs (Emerging Tech)

3.0 Fuzzy Models

Modelling and Imprecision
Fuzzy Sets Realization
Fuzziness and Big Data
Robotics and Drones

4.0 Systems Controls

Control and Fuzziness
Navigation, Guidance and Control
Systems (Direct/Indirect) and
    Models (Materials/Math
Robotics, Adaptive and Stochastic Controls
Control and AI

5.0 Artificial Intelligence

The transformation journey to AI
Enterprise Systems
Big Data and AI-The Interplay
The present and future of AI

6.0 Conclusions

Wrapping It All Up

He concluded by saying "These are just my early thoughts. I am expecting a rigorous update."

I had been planning to ask him how far he had gone with that book idea at the end of 2020. Unfortunately, I never got to ask him that question. I don't think he had completed the book. If he did, he would have informed me. If any of our publishing colleagues, particularly Professor Sunday Asaolu, Professor David Olowokere, Professor Abayomi Ajofoyinbo, and Dr. Babs Ayeni, are aware of this book project and the status of it, I would be interested in partnering to ensure that the book is completed in the honour of Professor Oyewusi Ibidapo-Obe. He deserves it. Similarly, if his Ijesha colleagues could move forward to complete his planned book on the History of Ijeshaland, it would be a lasting legacy in his memory. We will all miss Oye Ibidapo-Obe forever.

Appendix 2

The Intersection of Educational Development and Social Responsibility

Building a Sense of Responsibility
to Self, the Community, and the next Generation

Keynote Speech for
Baptist High School – Benin
Alumni In Diaspora

Gala Night: 30th July 2022

It is a great pleasure for me to have the opportunity to make a few comments about a topic that I cherish very much. The formal definition of responsibility refers to moral, legal, social, and mental accountability for one or more sets of expectations. The expectations may be established at the local level or at a global systems level. The expectations may range from self-centered ambitions, organizational goals, and community objectives to generational aspirations.

Legacy of Social Responsibility and Accountability

It is a wonderful life that we all enjoy. It is a life of joy when a child is born. It is a life of agony when a loved one departs. In between, there are triumphs and tribulations. One thing that is certain is the legacy that we leave behind. That legacy relates to our social responsibility to ourselves, our community, and the future generation. This means that everyone, whether young or old, can make a difference along the spectrum of responsibility and social accountability. In this regard, I offer the following quote as a guidance.

Together, we can accomplish.
United, we flourish.

Systems View of the World

We must take a systems view of the world and realize that what goes around comes around. Social isolation does not work in the long run. Prevention is better than correction. Advancement of the community is everyone's social responsibility. This implies the need for everyone to take on the social responsibility for everyone else, particularly the youth. The adage that "it takes a village to raise a child" has never been truer than in the present days of social uncertainties and inequities. Social stability and advancement of our society should be everyone's responsibility. We cannot afford to look the other way whenever we notice something that is not right or something that does not bode well for the welfare of the entire society. Social issues that we fail to address now may magnify into incidents that could adversely touch everyone in society, directly or indirectly. As individuals, we owe it to ourselves and our community to actively and directly participate in the resolution of problems in the society.

There is so much decadence evolving in our society nowadays. Many of these deplorable social issues manifest themselves in the form of criminal activities brought on by feelings of frustration, disenfranchisement, isolation, depression, desperation, and hopelessness. When members of our community are noticed to be facing family stress, financial discomfort, and despondency, it behooves all of us to jump in and offer helping hands. The offer of help can preempt serious socio-economic problems later on. If we do not help, minor problems may become big felonious incidents that may come back to touch us in unanticipated ways. A community may think it is safe by cocooning itself within the walls of its affluent neighborhood. I call this "social fencing." The reality is that no one can be completely insulated from crimes that occur within society. With freedom of movement and shrinking of geographical boundaries, crime importation and exportation should be a big concern for every one of us. We should all share in the collective responsibility of helping to preempt the evolution of social decadence so that we don't have to deal with the adverse results later. It is obvious that prisons have become a huge drain on society. Whether we want to accept it or not, we all pay for prisons. We pay in terms of loss of human capital, loss of loved ones, and impedance of economic growth. Wouldn't it be cheaper to institute programs that would preempt criminal tendencies and, consequently, reduce the need for more prisons?

Prevention is better than Correction

For social ills, preemption is far better than incarceration. Prevention is far better than correction. Proactive programs that help prevent crime are often cheap and accessible, such as offering social support to the less fortunate, providing a basis for optimism in youth, creating an atmosphere of belonging for everyone, offering encouragement, showing empathy where and when needed, and facilitating educational opportunities. For youth, support, discipline, and comfort are as much a responsibility of the parents as they are of everyone in the community. We are not all too far removed from the possible adverse impacts of juvenile delinquency.

Education is one sure way to advance society and minimize criminal tendencies. Where there is no education, there is a high potential for criminal activities. So, let us now band together to expand educational opportunities for everyone. This is exactly what Baptist High School Benin has done for decades. I am delighted that the Baptist High School Alumni in Diaspora, as a group, is carrying on this tradition both at home and abroad.

Hierarchy of Needs and Self Responsibility

The concept of "Hierarchy of Needs" proposed by Abraham Maslow in his 1943 paper, "A Theory of Human Motivation," still governs how we respond along the dimensions of our social expectations. This provides the premise of why I chose the topic for today's speech on building a sense of responsibility to self, community, and nation. A sense of responsibility to self is the foundation for accomplishing all other stages of expectations. In other words, we must fulfill our own ambitions before we can attend to higher-order expectations. Education and self-responsibility help us to accomplish this goal. A socially induced disparity in the hierarchy of needs implies that we may not be able to fulfill our responsibilities along the spectrum of self, community, and the next generation. Maslow's hierarchy of needs consists of five stages:

1. **Physiological Needs:** These are the needs for the necessities of life, such as food, water, housing, and clothing (i.e., Survival Needs). This is the level where access to money is most critical.
2. **Safety Needs:** These are the needs for security, stability, and freedom from physical harm (i.e., Desire for a safe environment).
3. **Social Needs:** These are the needs for social approval, friends, love, affection, and association (i.e., Desire to belong). For example, social belonging may bring about better economic outlook that may enable each

individual to be in a better position to meet his or her social needs.

4. **Esteem Needs:** These are the needs for accomplishment, respect, recognition, attention, and appreciation (i.e., Desire to be known).

5. **Self-Actualization Needs:** These are the needs for self-fulfillment and self-improvement (i.e., Desire to arrive). This represents the stage of opportunity to grow professionally and be in a position to selflessly help others.

To reach the top of Maslow's hierarchy of needs, we must display a sense of responsibility spanning self, community, and nation because no accomplishment occurs in isolation. Everything is interconnected. It is a systems world, and we must demonstrate a systems view of the world. What goes around comes around. We are all responsible for whatever happens in our community and our immediate work environment.

I want to share two of my favorite quotes with the audience this morning:

On the issue of getting involved, a Chinese quote says,

"Tell me and I forget;
Show me and I remember;
Involve me and I understand."

On the issue of diversity, I offer this quote,

"You don't really understand anything until you have looked at everything from many different perspectives."

In closing, please let us recognize that a good community is everyone's responsibility and a bad community is everyone's fault.

I am convinced and I have witnessed by Baptist High School – Benin Alumni in Diaspora is maintaining and advancing the commitment to social responsibility.

Thank you very much.

Appendix 3

Journal Articles of Interest in the Margin of Death

Fitting the cautionary theme of the margin of death in this book is a 2024 journal article by a team of authors: D. Gálvez-Pérez, B. Guirao, B., and A. Ortuño, who conducted an analysis of the elderly pedestrian traffic accidents in urban scenarios for the case of the Spanish municipalities. The authors found that as the elderly population grows, there is a greater concern for their safety on the roads. This is particularly important for elderly pedestrians who are more vulnerable to accidents. In Spain, one of the most aged countries in the world, the elderly accounted for 70% of all pedestrian deaths in 2019. In this study, the focus was on analyzing the occurrence of elderly pedestrian-vehicle collisions in Spanish municipalities and how it is related to the built environment. The study used the statistical technique of hurdle negative binomial model to analyze the number of elderly and non-elderly pedestrian accidents per municipality in 2016-2019. The exploratory analysis showed that cities with more than 50,000 inhabitants were safer for the elderly, and larger provincial capitals had lower elderly pedestrian traffic accident rates. The occurrence of all pedestrian traffic accidents was linked to the socio-demographic features. For elderly pedestrians, land use was found to be influential, with a lower proportion of land covered by manufacturing and service activities linked to a smaller number of accidents. Results showed that improving road safety for older pedestrians may not necessarily compromise the situation for the rest of population. Hence, policymakers should focus on infrastructure improvements adapted to the needs of elderly pedestrians. The reference for this study is provided below for the bold readers who want to explore this socially-motivated topic further:

Gálvez-Pérez, D., Guirao, B., & Ortuño, A. (2024). Analysis of the elderly pedestrian traffic accidents in urban scenarios: the case of the Spanish municipalities. *International Journal of Injury Control and Safety Promotion*, 1–20. https://doi.org/10.1080/17457300.2024.2335482

With this type of technical study that is socially focused, city planners, policy makers, and residents can work together to lessen the margin of death on city roads.

In another team-written journal article from 2010, P. Salmon, A. Williamson, M. Lenne, E. Mitsopoulos-Rubens, and C. M. Rudin-Brown, addressed systems-based accident analysis in the led outdoor activity domain, in which they present an application and evaluation of a risk management framework. Accidents represent a significant problem within the led outdoor activity domain. This article presents an evaluation of a risk management framework that can be used to understand such accidents and to inform the development of accident countermeasures and mitigation strategies for the led outdoor activity domain. Safety-compromising accidents occur regularly in the led outdoor activity domain. Formal accident analysis is an accepted means of understanding such events and improving safety. Despite this, there remains no universally accepted framework for collecting and analyzing accident data in the led outdoor activity domain. This article presents an application of Rasmussen's risk management framework to the analysis of the Lyme Bay sea canoeing incident. This involved the development of an Accimap, the outputs of which were used to evaluate seven predictions made by the framework. The Accimap output was also compared to an analysis using an existing model from the led outdoor activity domain. In conclusion, the Accimap output was found to be more comprehensive and supported all seven of the risk management framework's predictions, suggesting that it shows promise as a theoretically underpinned approach for analyzing, and learning from, accidents in the led outdoor activity domain. Here again, I present the reference citation for this important study that readers may explore further:

Salmon, P., Williamson, A., Lenné, M., Mitsopoulos-Rubens, E., & Rudin-Brown, C. M. (2010). Systems-based accident analysis in the led outdoor activity domain: application and evaluation of a risk management framework. *Ergonomics*, *53*(8), 927–939. https://doi.org/10.1080/001401 39.2010.489966

Printed in the United States
by Baker & Taylor Publisher Services